Words
That
Echo...

To Carol & Keith
With love

(signature) x
16·8·21

Paul Williams

Shield Crest

© Copyright 2021 Paul Williams

All rights reserved

ISBN: 978-1-913839-34-5

MMXXI

A CIP catalogue record for this
is available from the British Library

Published by
ShieldCrest Publishing Ltd.,
Aylesbury, Buckinghamshire,
HP18 0TF England
Tel: +44 (0) 333 8000 890
www.shieldcrest.co.uk

For Sharon (1967-2021)

INTRODUCTION

Almost 30 years ago I met my true love, my split-apart, the One.

During the first few months of our journey together I wrote, in a notebook, the words now presented here...
...words that speak of the hopes and dreams, the love and desire, the future and the fears...words of passion and waiting...and most of all, words of wanting...

...just wanting to be together, forever.

On 18th May 2021 my true love passed away.

A few weeks later I was sorting through some boxes and found a file containing the notebook, packed away to keep it safe. It had been there for almost 30 years.

I was hesitant to read it at first, expecting sadness. But later, in the garden with a beer and the sun, I read what I had written all those years ago; inevitably, sadness came and yet I realised that the words were just as relevant now as they had been before...the words echoed....

...the words echoed the love that we shared, echoed the past and the life that we shared ...and, as I sat there missing her so much, the words echoed the wanting...

...still just wanting to be together, forever.

I dedicate all these words to Sharon, my true love, my split-apart, the One.

BEGINNINGS

I'm originally from Birmingham and Sharon was born in Halifax (West Yorkshire); we both worked for the same organisation and met when our individual departments were moved from different locations into the same new premises (in a renovated mill).

The first time we spoke was beside a coffee machine (a cliche, but true) and it was an instant attraction although we did spend a lot of time becoming friends before either of us admitted it.

As time went on we got to the point where we just wanted to be together but there were things that needed to be sorted out and we had to be patient and wait. The pieces I wrote for Sharon in the original notebook, (which form the majority of the book) were written around this time, hence the themes of waiting and wanting.

Eventually we were together, as evidenced by the last few pieces in the book, written some months later than the first notebook.

We both loved music (not necessarily always the same music, but a lot of the same stuff); we both loved reading, Sharon was always great with words - song lyrics, poems, she did The Times Crossword every day; we just loved spending our time together.

I still live in West Yorkshire.

THANKS...

...to Sharon, obviously, for sharing her life with me, for being my best friend, for being my muse, for making me a better person...and for loving me.

...to you, the reader...I hope that you will recognise some, or all, of the feelings expressed here; I hope also that you have been, or will be, lucky enough to have shared the kind of love expressed.

...and I send my heartfelt thanks to Overgate Hospice (Elland, West Yorkshire) for looking after Sharon in her final days. You were, and are, truly wonderful.

DEDICATION

These words are for you, about you
About me, and about us.
They chart the growth of a spark
To a flame, to a fire,
To an inferno
Which is intense, and strong, and everlasting.

Though hopelessly inadequate
To fully express the true depth of our love
Keep these words forever

And if I´m not there to read them to you
Read them slowly to yourself
And if you feel down, or mad, or sad
I´ll read them to you.

For always they will be a reminder
Of the start of what will never end,
And I dedicate them to us.

PJW 1992

DREAMS (1)

I know there´s always love, I know what love is
It´s seldom found and often lost
Often undiscovered (don´t know where to look)
Or just left uncovered (don't want to look).

I´ve always been able to build up hopes,
I just couldn´t watch them being taken apart,
But the dreams were always my own.
Someone said put your hopes and dreams to one side
If you don´t, they get in the way of life
But if I lose sight of these,
Into, and out of, my peripheral vision
What is there left? (or right?)

Can obsession lead to possession, or to passion
Who knows?, always?, or probably?, (or never?)

And when love and hopes and dreams
And passion, obsession and possession are gone
Who or what or where do you and I turn?
To each other?, probably?, always?

MASK

I watch from the shadows at the back of the stalls, in a darkened theatre, long bereft of applause, as a figure with a mask stands alone on the stage, though it has no guests to entertain or critics to face.

The mask of the comedy is slowly lowered, removing the lips that break into a smile and, as the mask falls away, the figure's heart breaks open wide.

For this is its life, its true self, seeking no applause or ovation. This is no act, there are no lines to be said - but its movements, described in its motions, visibly portray its soul.

A board creaks and it echoes inside, like emotion let loose from within.

And I make my entrance from the back of the stalls.

PAIN

You wouldn´t believe how painful this little scratch is
I mean, scratches usually hurt for a short time
But I think this one will last a lot longer
Because this one is on my heart

POINT

What´s the point?

The sharp end
Of a needle?

Or the finger
Aimed at me
In accusation?

SAYING (1)

My Mom said...
"Let sleeping dogs lie"
But why shouldn't they be made to tell the truth.....
Like my sister and I

SAYING (2)

There's an old saying...
Let sleeping loves lie
Or let lying lovers sleep
Or let sleeping lovers sigh

WORDS (1)

Words in a dream
Forgotten by dawn
They seemed to make sense
Now they make none at all

  They all seemed so reasoned
  All felt so right
  Now reality´s back
  With the new morning light

    Did you share them with me?
    I wanted to know
    But now........
    I´m not so sure

LIKE

Like going to sea doesn´t make you a sailor
Being in love doesn´t make you a lover

Like climbing a hill doesn´t make you a king
Being alone doesn´t mean on your own

Like helping someone doesn´t make you a saint
Hearing a story doesn´t make you a judge

Like saving someone doesn´t make you a saviour
Being lost in the dark doesn´t mean it´s the night

Like a white lie doesn´t mean deceit
An honest opinion may not always be true

Like a tear unacknowledged,
                doesn´t mean "I don´t care"
Not always being there
                doesn´t mean "I´m not with you"

REMEMBER

And if ever there´s a next time
He´ll be sure to hold her tight
Just like the last time
On that cold and lonely night
A long way from home
In a room full of strangers
Where nobody´s known.

NIGHT

I lie awake all night sometimes
Thinking up poems and rhymes
Some of them I can remember in the morning
Others................................

DREAMS (2)

I know what hopes are,
You build them yourself and others take them apart,
But dreams are always your own.

I know what emotion is,
And I don´t know why,
But dreams are always your own.

I know what passion is,
It´s warm and shared and comes from inside,
But dreams are always your own.

I know what obsession is,
It wants everything and has nothing,
But dreams are always your own.

And I know what love is,
It´s seldom found and often lost,
But dreams are always your own.

ANSWER

You have brought a light into my life
    A daylight, lifting evening shadows
    from the corners of rooms that I had long since closed
Your words have lifted the covers
    And your eyes have looked directly
    into places where lie the feelings no-one knows.

Yes, I crouched and hid
    And tried, unsuccessfully,
    to express (or deny?) the truths and hurts and
    doubts
You have heard and seen that now
    And, somehow, knowing that you have shared it
    with me makes it so much better now.

Some things are supposedly for ever, others can never be at all
But I would rather have a part
Of something precious and special, than lose it altogether
For such things, like our friendship
Are so rare and so hard to discover.

Who knows the purpose or design of such things
    Why try to unravel such mysteries.
    Enjoy what we have found
    And let no-one, least of all ourselves,
    Take it away.

....

Too many people search and never find
Or don´t even know how or where to look
Or don´t even realise that they should
We know and have found each other,
And while it may not lead to a solution
It helps make our lives so good.

You rock me gently
While I cry over your words
Tears stain the page and blur my sight
You hold my hand tightly
As we lie together, with the answer,
In the depths of a dream, shrouded by night.

JOURNEY

As you prepare to leave the train, on which we are all
travelling,
I see, for the first time, the slight tremble in your hand
And the look in your eyes says "Where do I go from here?"
While your lips form around the words "I´m scared".

When the train stops, and you step from its security
I don´t want you to be lonely or alone
Must I watch from my window seat, or can I step down
Beside you, equally scarred and scared, and walk with you

To an unknown destination.

Don´t be scared, I know why you must leave this train
Don´t be scared, I understand why another journey calls you
Don´t be scared, turn around, I will be behind you
All of the way.
But the journey must be taken together.
Together all of the way from here.
For no-one will be our Samaritan on that other road

To an unknown destination.

Carry my wishes, hopes, dreams. And I´ll carry yours

To an unknown destination.

IF

If you can read the thoughts in my head,
Or look into my eyes,
You´ll know where I stand.

If blue skies thrill you once more,
Or a page filled with words,
You´ll know how I feel.

If you stare far into the distance,
But feel close to someone,
You´ll know where I am.

If you stretch out a supporting hand,
To steady me as I stumble,
You´ll know who I am.

If you feel warm on the inside,
As I lie above you,
You´ll know.

HELPLESS

I feel helpless
When I just want to call you
And I can´t
I feel helpless
When I just want to talk to you
And I can´t
I feel helpless
When I just want to reach out to you
And I can´t
I feel helpless
When I just want to hold your hand
And I can´t
I feel helpless
When I just want to say certain things to you
And I can´t
I feel helpless
When I just want to put my arms around you
And I can´t
I feel helpless
When I just want to hold you tight
And I can´t
I feel helpless
When I just want to hold you next to me
And I can´t
I feel helpless
When I just want to kiss you
And I can´t
I feel helpless
When I just want to caress you
And I can´t
We feel helpless

When we just want to make love
And we can´t....We feel helpless

When you aren´t there
Next to me, with me,
Holding me, hugging me, loving me
I feel helpless
And I cry
Deep inside
For I can´t cry aloud
And you know
I feel helpless.

BREEZE

I have lain with you
'Neath the stars and the sun
Felt your heartbeat next to mine
Felt your cool breath on my cheek
And your arms held tight around me

As each we listened
To the soft summer breeze
Trying to pass between us
But it cannot
For we are too close.

MOMENT

Never wanted average, or the doubt it brings,
Never wanted a number one or the two point four,
Who wants to be the man at the top
When they just want to see you fall

Although a man can dream a thousand times
Of a thousand things to do,
The only thing I want to do right now
Is to spend my time with you.

Never wanted to compensate, for the things I should have
done
Got backed into a corner, trapped with feelings such as
these,
They expected the world in their search for truth
Got dragged down, but never missed

And though a man can dream a thousand times
Of a thousand things to do
Of all the things I should not be
I want to be with you.

Never wanted to be held so tight, as I do when darkness
falls,
I won´t want that first night to end, nor the sun to climb
the skies,
The touch of your hand on my skin
The look of love in your eyes

And though a man can dream a thousand times
Of a thousand things to do
The nearest thing to dreaming
Is a moment spent with you.

WAITING

As I count the hours
Until I know I will see you again
(19 ½ to go)
I am close to tears and I ache inside
For such is the intensity that I feel

I hug myself, willing sleep to come
To come quickly and end my despair
Let me sleep deep and long
Where dreams are real and
You are real, and we are one

Delay my awakening
For I know when it comes
The hours that pass speedily
While I sleep
Will slow to an agonising crawl

(19) and I'm dying inside
They stretch out before me
Like a desert
And all I want is to hold you
While we exchange our gifts to each other

Take the gift of my love for you
And hold it forever, where you will always know
What you mean to me
Because I want to show you
Day by day, every day

....

This is now, I can't think further
Than (18 ½) hours; and the few fleeting hours that will
follow
I know they will leave without staying
For more than a few minutes
Then the wait will begin again for another tomorrow

Make "tomorrows" into "todays"
And leave "yesterdays" behind
Only then will the waiting end
And living begin
And loving you, you loving me

TIME

Time - you are a real bastard
You slow to a crawl
When I need you to race by
Minutes stretched into hours
That last a lifetime
And then you accelerate to full speed
When I need you to stop
When I have only a few hours
To be with my love
You condense them into nothing
You mean sod
But I'll get my own back
When my love is by my side
It will be forever
And then you'll be redundant

WORDS (2)

Words have abandoned me now
Fled this page
Only those that I captured
And committed to a sentence remain,
Until you read them, release them
And give them freedom and life

QUESTIONS

Why me?
>Why you?
>>Choice?
>>>Or fate?

DIRECT

I seem always to write in questions or riddles
Seldom getting to the point, or,
Disguising it
In such a way that it becomes lost or unfathomable

So, for once, I´ll write direct
And say
I love you and want you to be with me always

HOPE

There are some things in life
That should be...

...continuous, but get disrupted or broken

Others should last but a short time
But seem to carry on endlessly,
Regardless of time, space or emotion

All that I can hope for is to find
Something that I want to last
For always and that will never succumb
To the pressures placed upon it by me, you or the
world

RIDE

We´re rushing headlong
On this roller coaster ride
Scared out of our wits
Wanting somewhere to hide
Clinging to each other
Excitement taking over
With each twist and turn
Within each other we take cover
Fleeting darkness, into light
A short brief respite
Another corner, another bend
Neither wanting this ride to end

WHERE?

It´s in the way your eyes
Hold mine for a moment
Smiling, laughing, loving
All translated then into your smile
Lighting up both our faces, with not a word spoken

It´s in the way your touch,
So gentle and tender on my face
Says so much
Sending messages that explain
How much you care, and lingers long after you have
gone

It´s in the way your kisses
Meet mine and say
So sweetly, so strongly,
What your lips have tried to say
When somehow the words don´t seem sufficient

It´s in your looks
Though you deny it
It´s in your thoughts
And how you know
What we both want to be....

It´s in these that I see your love

CHANGE

Once we were just friends
With lively conversation
In the company of others
Two of a kind in the world

I don´t remember when it happened
I can´t pinpoint a moment
But a spark became a flame
And we became a part of each other

Now, we are lovers
The conversations are personal
And we seek to be alone together
Away from the world

BEST

I tried to think
About the best part
Of loving you
But there are too many reasons to choose from

I tried to think
About the thing I like
Best about you
But the list was endless, all the choices equal

I'm just glad to have you near me
And that we love each other

OPPOSITES

The feelings that I have
When I´m not with you
Are exactly the opposite to those
That I have when we´re together

LATER

A couple of weeks after I found the notebook I came across another small file with a few additional pieces written for Sharon.

"Weather" was almost certainly written at the same time as the other pieces in the notebook, but for some reason, long forgotten, it never made it into the notebook.

The rest of the pieces are from some months later that same year, by which time we were actually, properly, together.....I think it shows....

WEATHER

Sat in a car at the top of a hill
Wanting words to come easier than this
While the rain lashed the windows
And the wind rocked our world
...And we talked about the weather

Tentatively exploring each other's thoughts
Looking for reasons to stay, not to go
But while the barriers receded
And the inhibitions fell away
...We still talked about the weather

Now the darkness has fallen
And the world looks a different place
In the light of our love
Reflected in the rain
...Who gives a damn about the weather

COMPLETE

Trailing red lights in the dark,
Mile after mile, my only thoughts
Are of getting home to you, where you are.
Though it´s only a day,
Time spent away from you still passes too slow

Watching daytime TV,
Mind-numbingly dull and inane, my only thoughts
Are of you sitting, working, not wanting to be there,
A short distance away.
But still time passes slow, till you say "I´m finished"

Sitting in the dark,
Hoping you are having a good time
But missing you nevertheless, no less, more.
They said that this would pass or fade, but it hasn´t

Being in love with you, and being with you,
Make my life, make me, complete.

SUN

You said you didn´t like the sun
It gave you prickly heat you said
But you sat in the sun with me, For a while,
(When it got too hot we went to bed).

SPECIAL

There's a special place
That we go to, you and I
We're there every night
And it's full
Of love, and hugs, and kisses
And of holding each other.

It's the best place in the world
And given the choice
I would stay there, forever,
Never venturing out
Into the outside

But we both want to stay,
For without each other it's just a "place"
Only together can a "place", or a time, or an event
have any meaning at all

But best of all is that special place
In the dark of the night
In the light of our love

TOGETHER

Hands hold
Lips kiss
Fingers caress
Legs entwine
Voices speak
Bodies touch
Arms hold
And we´re together.

Fingers join
Lips kiss
Hands caress
Legs entwine
Voices speak
Bodies touch
Arms hold
And we´re together again.

FIRST

Christmas Day had come and gone
Presents wrapped and then unwrapped
Frequently you fingered the gift
Hung around your neck
And in quiet moments we smiled
Enjoying the love we shared

We walked out to where the mist hung low
And the ice was strong enough
To hold the weight of thrown stones
Where, hand in hand,
We passed the place where once we kissed
A moment we could only steal

Such moments are no longer borrowed
Nor stolen
These moments are ours alone
And make up the life we share
But I shall never forget
The first Christmas that was ours together

RIGHT

When I was alone,
And I couldn´t see you, to tell you things,
I had to write them down

But now we are together,
And I don´t have to write anything down
Anymore.

CODA (1): WORDS

Sharon loved words...song lyrics, poetry, The Times, (and The Times Crossword) and she was never without a book to read.

At the time of the notebook, she sent me a postcard with just a quote on the back...

"You'll never see that you had all of me. You'll never see the poetry you stirred in me"

Kate Bush "The Saxophone Song" (1978)

And in her final letter to me in May 2021 she included the following...

"I will pass my days within the sound of your voice, and my nights within the reach of your hand.
And none shall come between us"

William Nicholson "Slaves of the Mastery" (2001)

CODA (2): MUSIC

Music was always a huge part of our lives together. The words of "Moment" became the basis of a song that I wrote for Sharon in 1992, re-titled "A Man Can Dream", which remains recorded, but unreleased.

At a very early stage in our journey together, around the time of writing the words collected in the notebook, I picked up a guitar and sang Sharon a song: "Please Be With Me" by Eric Clapton (from the 1974 album "461 Ocean Boulevard"). She loved it and it kind of became "our song" (although she always called it Gypsy).

If you can, have a quick listen to "Please Be With Me".......

......I wish she could be with me right now...

BV - #0068 - 100821 - C0 - 210/148/3 - PB - 9781913839345 - Gloss Lamination